Sin... ...ve been
dito... ...instead
(and... ...y, Finally,
bookse... ...nning new
prod... ...ders back . . .

THE BEANO

JOKE BOOK

If y

SQUELCH!

WARNING! BORING GROWN-UP STUFF BELOW!

PUFFIN BOOKS

Published by the Penguin Group
Penguin Books Ltd, 80 Strand, London WC2R 0RL, England
Penguin Group (USA) Inc., 375 Hudson Street, New York, New York 10014, USA
Penguin Group (Canada), 90 Eglinton Avenue East, Suite 700, Toronto, Ontario, Canada M4P 2Y3
Penguin Ireland, 25 St Stephen's Green, Dublin 2, Ireland (a division of Penguin Books Ltd)
Penguin Group (Australia), 707 Collins Street, Melbourne, Victoria 3008, Australia
Penguin Books India Pvt Ltd, 11 Community Centre, Panchsheel Park, New Delhi – 110 017, India
Penguin Group (NZ), 67 Apollo Drive, Rosedale, Auckland 0632, New Zealand
Penguin Books (South Africa) (Pty) Ltd, Block D, Rosebank Office Park, 181 Jan Smuts Avenue,
Parktown North, Gauteng 2193, South Africa

Penguin Books Ltd, Registered Offices: 80 Strand, London WC2R 0RL, England

puffinbooks.com

First published 2013. This edition published 2014.
001

With contributions by Dan Newman, Ruth Reyes and The Beano readers

The Beano ®© and associated characters TM © DC Thomson & Co. Ltd. 2014
All rights reserved

Printed in Great Britain by Clays Ltd, St Ives plc

British Library Cataloguing in Publication Data
A CIP catalogue record for this book is available from the British Library

ISBN: 978-0-141-35596-2

www.greenpenguin.co.uk

THE BEANO

JOKE BOOK

PUFFIN

CONTENTS

WELCOME . . .

. . . to The Beano's chortlesome, guffaw-tastic, titter-worthy joke book!

A lot can happen in 75 years. Since 1938, man has landed on the moon, the internet has been invented and your dear old grandad has got really, really, REALLY wrinkly. But one thing that's been ever-present is *The Beano*, delivering a weekly dose of laughs from Dennis the Menace, Lord Snooty and everyone else in between.

To celebrate, we've put together this collection of our favourite funnies – and a few of your own, too! That's right – as you make your way through the pages that follow, you'll see that we've picked out a gaggle of gags given to us by you, our trusty readers.

So sit back, set your funny bones to seriously tickled, and enjoy. Then, once you've reached the end, maybe you could think about what will be making us all laugh 75 years from now. Lasers, robots and hologram custard is our guess.

In 1938 . . .

 There was very little on TV. Hardly anything, in fact. Seriously, in those days they didn't even have The Massive Elephant Channel or Pie TV. Can you imagine? And just a year later, BBC TV was suspended completely because of World War II.

 A radio show based on *The War of the Worlds* sci-fi book caused panic when listeners mistook it for news of a real-life alien invasion. Oops.

 Italy won the third-ever Football World Cup, which was hosted by France. Argentina and Uruguay went off in a huff and decided not to play because they weren't happy about it being held in Europe for the second time in a row.

 Superman made his comic debut. He's sort of like Bananaman, but with a less impressive jawline.

 A train called Mallard set a new world speed record for steam, at 125.88 mph. By way of comparison, that's almost as fast as Billy Whizz can move when it's been a long day and he's feeling a bit tired.

 Seabiscuit won a famous horse race at Pimlico Race Course in Baltimore, Maryland. It sounds quite impressive, until you find out that Seabiscuit was actually a horse, and not a biscuit. But just imagine if he'd been a biscuit! Wow! He'd have been the best biscuit ever (other than perhaps a chocolate digestive?).

 On 30th July, the first ever issue of *The Beano* came out! 'Hurrah!' cried pretty much anyone with any sense.

MENACE FUNNIES

Laugh - or else!

GASSY FIZZ

Dennis tried squashing some cans of pop, but he had to stop.
It was soda pressing!

Dennis was getting a lift from Dad, but he couldn't remember how to fasten his seatbelt.
Suddenly it clicked!

Mum's making a reversible jumper for Dennis.
He's looking forward to seeing how it turns out!

Dennis made a wooden go-kart, with wooden wheels and a wooden seat.
It wooden go!

Gnasher's Canine Cackles

What do you get when you cross a dog with a telephone?
A golden receiver!

Why don't dogs make good dancers?
Because they have two left feet!

How did the little Scottish dog feel when he saw a monster?
Terrier-fied!

How do you find a lost dog in the woods?
Press your ear against a tree and listen for the bark!

What happened when Gnasher ate nothing but garlic?
His bark was much worse than his bite!

How do you stop a dog from smelling?
Put a peg on its nose!

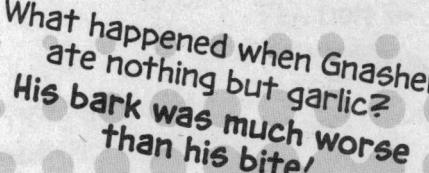

When does a dog go 'moo'?
When it's learning a new language!

GNASH!

What kind of dog sniffs out new flowers?
A bud hound!

MINX MAYHEM

Minnie gets back on her bike every time she falls off.
She always re-cycles!

Minnie's learning to juggle.
She's OK, but if she tries with more than three objects, things get out of hand!

Minnie lost her temper while she was doing gymnastics.
She completely flipped!

Minnie visited Little Plum and ended up in charge of the whole tribe.
She's a little miss-chief!

Minnie was really annoyed when her parents didn't buy her the expensive rollerblades she wanted.
What cheapskates!

'Mum, how did you know I hadn't washed my face?'
'Easy, Minnie. You forgot to wet the soap this time!'

Minnie's best ever present was a set of drums.
Every week, Dad gives her money not to play them!

Minnie couldn't remember how to throw a boomerang.
Eventually it came back to her!

The Bash Street Kids'
classroom capers

Teacher: How can we keep the school clean?
Plug: By staying at home!

Sidney: Is it wrong to punish someone for something they haven't done?
Teacher: Of course it is!
Sidney: OK then. I haven't done my homework!

Teacher: Can anyone make up a sentence using the word 'lettuce'?
Spotty: 'Lettuce' out of school early!

Why did Teacher have to turn the lights on?
Because his class was so dim!

What happened to the plant in maths class?
It grew square roots!

Why was the maths book always unhappy?
Because it had a lot of problems!

What did zero say to eight?
Nice belt!

WINSTON THE CAT'S Purrfect Puns!

Winston left the vacuum cleaner running while he slept.
It was an overnight suck-cess!

Winston only uses the best stuff to clean the school.
It's really soaper!

Winston drank a bowl of milk in record time.
He set a new lap record!

What's the opposite of a flabby tabby?
An itty bitty kitty!

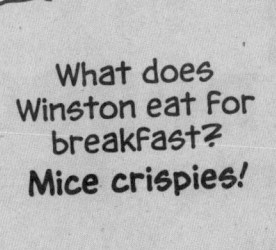

What does Winston eat for breakfast?
Mice crispies!

What does Winston read while he's eating?
The mewspaper!

Did you hear about the cat that ate a ball of wool?
She had mittens!

What happened when Winston swallowed a pound coin?
There was some money left in the kitty!

Where does Winston get his cleaning supplies?
From a cat-alogue!

FLOUR

ROGER
THE DODGER'S
Random Rib-

What do you get if you cross a frog with a rabbit? **Ribbits!**

Where do mice park their boats? **At the hickory dickory dock!**

Why wouldn't the tiny prawn share his treasure? **Because he was a little shellfish!**

'Dad, there's someone at the door collecting for a new swimming pool.'
'Give him a glass of water!'

'Do you want a wonder watch? It only costs a pound.'
'Why's it called a wonder watch?'
'Because every time you look at it, you'll wonder what the time is!'

Roger has a big rubber band tied to his camera.
It's handy for quick snaps!

What's green and furry, has four legs and can't swim?
A pool table!

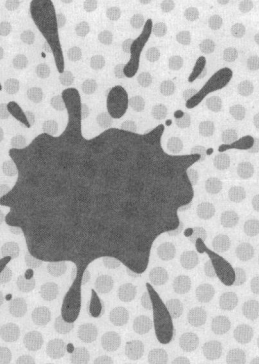

What's green and furry, has four legs and is extremely dangerous?
A pool table with woodworm!

Angel Face's
NOT-REMOTELY-ANGELIC
Laughs

Angel Face demanded a go at playing cricket. She was a big hit!

Knock, knock!
Who's there?
Boo.
Boo who?
Aw, don't cry – it's only me!

Why are you wearing loud shoes?
So that my feet won't fall asleep!

What do you say to a hitchhiker with one leg?
Hop in!

What kind of hair do oceans have?
Wavy!

Football Funnies

First Half!

Why did the footballer take a piece of rope on to the pitch?
He was the skipper!

Where do footballers dance?
At the foot-ball!

Which football team
loves ice-cream?
Aston Vanilla!

What tea do
footballers drink?
Penaltea!

What did the
bumblebee
striker say?
Hive scored!

How do you stop
squirrels from playing
football in the garden?
**Hide the ball – it drives
them nuts!**

Why should you
be careful when
playing against a
team of big cats?
**They might be
cheetahs!**

Where do spiders
play their annual
cup final?
Webley Stadium!

23

Smiffy's Random RIB-TICKLERS

What do fish
call a submarine?
A can of people!

Why can't you take a
picture of a pirate with
a wooden leg?
**Because a wooden leg
doesn't take pictures!**

Why was the piano
on the porch?
**Because it forgot
its keys!**

What did the tie
say to the hat?
**You go on ahead
and I'll hang
around!**

When do cows
make a noise?
**When they're in
the moo'd!**

Two mobile phones got married.
They exchanged ringtones . . . but the reception was terrible!

Why are eggs useless at telling jokes?
They keep cracking up!

How do you make an octopus laugh?
Give it ten-tickles!

Billy Whizz's
EXTRA-QUICK
One-Liners

He who laughs last
. . . probably didn't
get the joke!

I was born to
be a pessimist.
My blood type
is B Negative!

I went to the canteen and
ordered a light lunch. They
served me three candles
and a bulb!

I find it difficult to make
friends because of my
addiction to pasta. I'm
mostly OK, although it
does get cannelloni!

I bet Dracula does all his shopping online, just so he can keep clicking on 'your account'!

Two silkworms had a race. It ended in a tie!

I thought the tube of superglue I got for my birthday was a lousy present, but now I'm quite attached to it!

The local baker has stopped making ring doughnuts. He says he's tired of the hole thing!

Dennis' Dad's Garden Gags

Why did the butterfly get a mobile phone?
She wanted to cauliflower!

What do you call a country where people only drive pink cars?
A pink carnation!

What were King Tut's favourite flowers?
Chrysanthemummies!

What kind of flower grows on your face?
Tulips!

What kind of tree can
fit in your hand?
A palm tree!

Knock, knock!
Who's there?
Leaf!
Leaf who?
Leaf me alone!

...ARGHH! A PEA! A PEA
WENT IN! ARGHH!

What did the big flower
say to the small flower?
What's up, bud?

What do you call a girl
with a frog in her hair?
Lily!

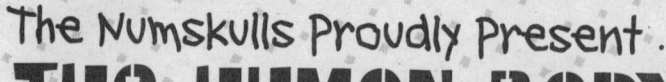

The Numskulls Proudly Present....
THE HUMAN BODY!

What part of the body does even the most careful person overlook?
The nose!

What's the most musical bone?
The trom-bone!

What do you call a lady with one leg shorter than the other?
Eileen!

What makes music in your hair?
A head band!

31

READERS' JOKES
Part One

We asked for them – and you delivered! So if these gags aren't funny, you've only got yourself to blame! Don't say we didn't warn you ...

What do you call a deer with no eyes?
No eye-deer!
Shaneese, 9

What wobbles in the sky?
A jellycopter!
Lydia, 5

What do you call a man with a piece of wood on his head?
Edwood!
Eve, 11

What do you call an electric parrot?
A shock-a-too!
Archie, 6

How do monkeys
cook their toast?
**They stick it under
the gorilla!**
Trudy Violet, 3

What's black and white
and red all over?
A sunburned penguin!
Harriet, 9

Why couldn't anyone
phone the zoo?
**Because the lions
were busy!**
Evie, 8

How do you get
Pikachu on the bus?
Poke-him-on!
Lily, 7

Where's a rodent's favourite
place to go on holiday?
Hamsterdam!
Sonny, 8

What do you
call two rows
of cabbages?
**A dual
cabbage-way!**
Philippa, 10

Calamity James'
Top 13 Unfortunate Doctor, Doctor Jokes (Part One)

'Doctor, doctor, have you got anything for a bad headache?'

'Of course. Just take this hammer and hit yourself on the head. Then you'll have a bad headache!'

'Doctor, doctor, I keep seeing double.'

'Just lie down on the couch.'

'Which one?'

'Doctor, doctor, I need something for my kidneys.'

'Here's a pound of steak – make yourself a pie!'

'Doctor, doctor, I've broken my leg. What shall I do?'

'Limp!'

'Doctor, doctor, my mind keeps wandering.'
'Don't worry – it's too weak to get very far!'

James went to see the doctor.
'Doctor,' he said. 'I've eaten something that disagrees with me.' A voice from inside his stomach said, 'No, you haven't!'

'Doctor, doctor, will this ointment clear up my spots?'
'I never make rash promises!'

Little Plum's
Little Fun

What is a tornado's
favourite game?
Twister!

'Have you ever had an accident, Chief?'
'No, Plum. Never.'
'Really? What about when that
rattlesnake bit you?'
**'That wasn't an accident –
he bit me on purpose!'**

Little Plum rode his horse up to the
stagecoach, leapt in through the window,
climbed out of the other side on to the
roof, whistled for his horse to come
round, jumped on its back and rode away.
'What on earth was that about?' asked
one of the passengers.
'Nothing really,' said the driver. 'It's just a
stage he's going through!'

Chief found Plum kneeling down with one ear pressed to the ground.

'There's a herd of cattle a mile away, Chief,' said Plum. 'Two hundred cows, with six cowboys on brown horses and three cowboys on black horses.'

'Wow, you can tell all that just by listening to the ground?' said the Chief.

'No, they ran over my head,' groaned Plum!

What does a cloud wear under his raincoat? Thunderwear!

BANANAMAN'S
FRUITY FUNNIES

Why did the banana go
to the doctor?
**Because it wasn't
peeling well!**

Harry, 8

What do you give
a sick lemon?
Lemon aid!

What is a scarecrow's
favourite fruit?
Straw-berries!

Why was the
strawberry sad?
**Because its mum was
in a jam!**

Why was the orange
left on its own?
**Because the
banana split!**

What's worse than finding
a worm in your apple?
**Finding half a worm in
your apple!**

Knock, knock!
Who's there?
Figs.
Figs who?
Figs the doorbell,
its broken!

MAZOOF!

I saw Bananaman with bananas mashed over his face and smeared all down his costume.
I don't think he's eating properly!

Gran's Giggles

'I'm worried I'm starting to lose my memory.'
'Really, Gran? When did this start?'
'When did what start?'

'What's that you're putting on your face, Gran?'
'Wrinkle cream.'
'Wow, it's really good at making them!'

'Finally, everything's starting to click for me,' said Gran. 'My knees, my elbows, my neck . . .'

Dennis visited Gran and scoffed his way through a bowl of peanuts she'd left for him on the table.

'Thanks for the nuts, Gran,' he said as he left.

'No – thank you, Dennis,' Gran replied. 'While my false teeth are being fixed all I can do is suck the chocolate off!'

'Wow, well done on blowing out all your birthday candles, Gran!'

'Well, I had to be quick – my glasses were starting to melt!'

Three old geezers were walking in the park.

'Windy, isn't it?' said one.

'No, it's Thursday,' said the second.

'Me too,' said the third. 'Let's go and have a cup of tea!'

'Where were you born, Gran?'

'Beanotown.'

'Really – what part?'

'All of me.'

'Have you lived here all your life?'

'Not yet!'

41

RASHER'S
Bacon Banter

What are pigs warned to look out for in big cities?
Pig-pockets!

Why didn't the piglets listen to their teacher?
Because he was an old boar!

Why did the pig go to the amusement arcade?
To play the slop machine!

Why should you never play football with pigs?
Because they always hog the ball!

What are Rasher's favourite jokes?
One-loiners!

Rasher ate ten jars of marmalade.
He was jam-packed!

Why did the piglets do badly in school?
They were all slow loiners!

Why did the little pig hide the soap?
He heard the farmer yell 'hogwash!'

I don't believe Rasher could eat a whole bin full of rubbish.
That's a load of trash!

BASH STREET BRAIN-TEASERS

How do we know that the
Earth won't come to an end?
Because it's round!

What's a myth?
A female moth!

Who invented fire?
Some bright spark!

How was the Roman
Empire divided?
With a pair of Caesars!

Who invented fractions?
Henry the $1/8$!

How did Vikings
communicate?
By Norse code!

What's a forum?
Two-um plus two-um!

Where is Hadrian's Wall?
Around Hadrian's garden!

Who made King Arthur's
round table?
Sir Cumference!

READERS' JOKES

Part Two

What do elves do
after school?
Gnomework!

Barney, 5

What do you get if you paint
a whole house in one day?
An aching arm!

Ivy, 9

Where do eggs
go to live?
New Yolk!

Andie, 9

Who is Andy Murray's favourite
cartoon character?
Tennis the Menace!

Eva, 8

What did the elephant
say to the pig about
the camel?
He's got the hump!

Aimee, 6

A panda walks into a bar, eats some food and then squirts the manager with a water pistol. Outside, he is stopped by the police, who ask him why he did it. The panda says, 'Look me up in the dictionary.'

They do. It says, 'Eats shoots and leaves.'

Carlotta and Lois, 8 and 6

Why did the man take a pencil to bed?
To draw the curtains!

James, 4

Why did the doughnut go to the dentist?
To get a chocolate filling!

Vaibhav, 9

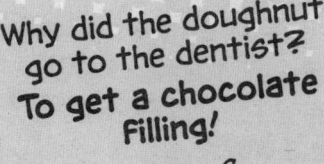

Did you hear about the scarecrow that won a Nobel Prize?
He was out standing in his field!

Jack, 12

What do you call a dog that loves bubble bath?
A shampoodle!

Romy, 5

What is the most romantic fruit?
The passion fruit!

Mabli, 9

DENNIS FUNNIES

Dennis isn't sure his parents have much idea about raising children.

They keep sending him to bed when he's wide awake, and waking him up when he's sleepy!

'I don' t think I should go to school today, I don't feel well.'

'Oh dear Dennis, where don't you feel well?'

'In school!'

Dennis threw a pile of tomatoes with his eyes closed.

He didn't know what he was missing!

'Dad, why are you standing on the computer?'

'I'm surfing the internet, of course!'

How did Dennis feel after pretending to be Gnasher?

Rrruff!

'Why are you so late coming home, Dennis?'

'I was helping an old man cross the road.'

'That's nice of you - but why did it take so long?'

'He didn't want to go!'

49

GNASHER'S
Gnice Jokes

What do you call Gnasher
when he sits in a muddy
ditch by the road?
A mutt in a rut!

Where does Gnasher sit
in the cinema?
Anywhere he likes!

What should you do if
your dog eats
your pen?
Use a pencil instead!

How does Gnasher get
off a boat?
He disem-barks!

Where do Eskimos
train their dogs?
In the mush-room!

Gnasher dressed up as a postman for Halloween.
He bit himself!

Which side of Gnasher has the most hair?
The outside!

What's it called when you have too many dogs?
A roverdose!

Gnasher wandered into a performance by a flea circus.
He stole the show!

Fatty Hates Fruit
(and isn't too keen on veg either)

What school subject
is the fruitiest?

**History, because it's full
of dates!**

What did one sunbathing
banana say to the other
sunbathing banana?

I don't know about you,
but I'm beginning to peel!

What are twins'
favourite fruit?
Pears!

What's small, red
and whispers?
A hoarse radish!

How does a monster
eat an apple?
By goblin it!

What is a vampire's
favourite fruit?
A neck-tarine!

What kind of fruit can
fix your sink?
A plum-ber!

Why did the man lose
his job at the orange
juice factory?
**Because he couldn't
concentrate!**

Why are grapes never lonely?
**Because they come in
bunches!**

THE 3 BEARS
Grin and Bear It!

What do you call bears with no ears?
B!

'Who's been eating my porridge?' squeaked Ted Bear.
'Who's been eating my porridge?' grumbled Ma Bear.
'Is there any more porridge?' burped Pa Bear.

What should you call Pa Bear when he starts to lose his hair?
Fred Bear!

What's brown, furry and goes 'RRRRG'?
A bear walking backwards!

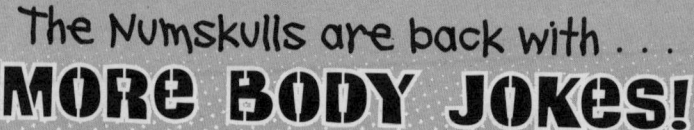

The Numskulls are back with . . .
MORE BODY JOKES!

Contact lenses are
easy to lose.
You need to keep
your eye on them!

 When should you cut
your nails?
Before they get
out of hand!

Why didn't the skeleton
cross the road?
It didn't have
the guts!

'Have you got any holes in your pants?'
'No, of course not!'
'How do you get your legs in them, then?'

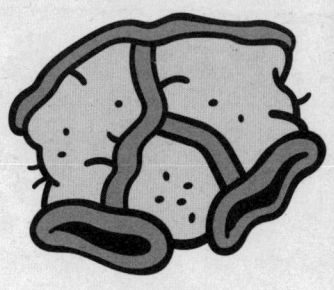

Why are tall people never tired?
They sleep longer!

Edd isn't really that fond of soap.
There's no need to rub his face in it though!

What has one eye but cannot see?
A needle!

I don't think I need a spine.
It's holding me back!

BABY BEA'S Biggest & BEST ...

Tiny Titters

How does a baby ghost cry?
BOO-hoo!

Mum: Why is there a strange baby in the crib?
Daughter: You told me to change the baby!

Mum: Would you rather have a baby brother or a baby sister?
Son: I'd rather have a jelly baby!

What did Baby Corn say to Mum Corn?
Where's Pop Corn?

Knock, knock!
Who's there?
Baby owl.
Baby owl who?
Baby owl see you later, or baby not!

How do you get a baby astronaut to sleep?
You rocket!

How can you tell if a snake is a baby snake?
It has a rattle!

Why were ancient Egyptian children so confused?
Because their daddies were mummies!

Babyface stole a case of soap from the store.
He made a clean getaway!

Roger the Dodger's
ROTTEN RIDDLES

Why is it so difficult
to open a piano?
**Because all the
keys are inside!**

What cheese is
made backwards?
Edam!

What runs but
never walks?
Water!

What can you make
that can't be seen?
A noise!

How many rotten
eggs does it take
to make a
stink bomb?
A phew!

What do ghosts use
to clean their hair?
Sham-boo!

MEGA STINK BOMB

Where do you go
when you flush
yourself down
the toilet?
Waterloo!

What happens
when you throw
a green pebble in
the Red Sea?
It gets wet!

TAUNTING TEACHER

Teacher gets compliments every time he parks his car.

Well, someone keeps leaving him notes saying 'Parking Fine'!

'You can't sleep in my class, Danny!'

'I know. Do you think you could talk a little quieter?'

'I don't think I deserved zero for this test, Sir.'

'Neither do I, Smiffy. But apparently I couldn't give you anything lower!'

'Danny, why are you telling everyone I'm an idiot?'

'Sorry, sir, I didn't know it was a secret!'

'You copied Danny's homework, didn't you, Plug?'

'Er, yes. How did you know?'

'Where Danny put "I don't know", you put, "Me neither"!'

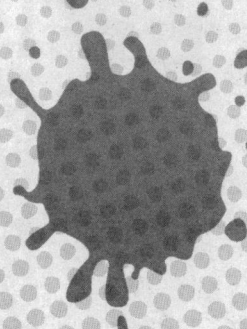

'You'll be pleased to hear we've only got half a day of school this morning.'

'Yaayy!'

'We'll have the other half a day this afternoon.'

'You're not paying much attention, Toots. Do you have trouble with your hearing?'

'What? No, Sir. Just with listening to you!'

'Sir, what's the difference between wages and a salary?'

'They're both money you get for working, but wages are paid weekly, while a salary is paid monthly. For instance, I get a salary.'

'Really, Sir? Where do you work?'

MIRTHTASTIC MINNIE

'Oh no! Fatty has just fallen down the wishing well!'
'Wow – it actually works!'

What's the difference between a storm cloud and Minnie with toothache?
One pours with rain, the other roars with pain!

'Cheer up, Minnie. Try what I do – when I'm down in the dumps, I get some new clothes.'
'I always wondered where you got them from, Mum!'

'They're really mean at that chip shop. I hate them!'
'Why's that, Minnie?'
'I just heard they batter their fish!'

'You know how people point at their wrist when they want to know the time?'

'Yes, Minnie. So what?'

'Well, why don't they point to their bums when they want to know where the toilet is?'

What do you get from Minnie when she's in a bad mood?
As far away as possible!

'Can you help me with this homework, Dad?'

'I'm not sure, Minnie. It wouldn't be right, would it?'

'Probably not, but have a go anyway!'

Minnie fell asleep with one eye open.
She didn't sleep a wink!

GNIPPER'S
BITE-SIZED GAGS

Gnipper used to have a fear
of speed bumps.
He's slowly getting over it!

What are dog biscuits
made from?
Collie-flour!

What did the hungry Dalmation say when he'd finished eating?
That hit the spots!

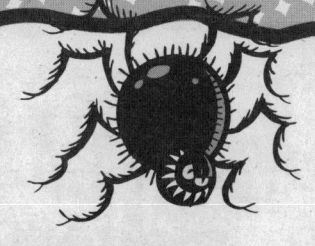

What should you do if Gnipper starts chewing a dictionary?
Take the words right out of his mouth!

What's Gnipper's favourite pizza?
Pupperoni!

Why did Gnipper cross the road twice?
He was trying to fetch a boomerang!

How does Gnipper stop a video from playing?
He presses paws!

Why does Gnipper wag his tail?
Well, who else is going to do it for him?

FOOTBALL FUNNIES

Second Half!

What's the chilliest ground
in the Premier League?
Cold Trafford!

Playing five-a-side football at
lunchtime, I wondered why the
ball was getting bigger.
Then it hit me!

What did the football say
to the footballer?
I get a kick out of you!

Why are football
grounds odd?
**Because you can sit in
the stands but can't
stand in the sits!**

What is the bank
manager's favourite
type of football?
Fiver side!

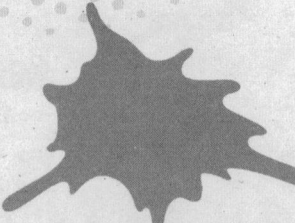

What part of a football pitch smells nicest?
The scenter spot!

Why did the footballer hold his boot to his ear?
Because he liked sole music!

Why are football players never asked out for dinner?
Because they're always dribbling!

READERS' JOKES
part Three

What do you call a
man with a seagull on
his head?
Cliff!
What do you call a
man under a car?
Jack!

Eve, 11

Knock, knock!
Who's there?
Scott.
Scott who?
**Scott nothing to do
with you!**

Georgia, 8

What did the
policeman say to
his stomach?
**You're under a
vest!**

Laura, 11

What do you say
if you get your
punctuation wrong?
Dash!

Molly, 11

Why did the crab blush?
It saw the ship's bottom!
Luc, 8

What did the Greek cheese say when he looked in the mirror?
Halloumi!
Mieke, 5

Why don't people like Bob Marley's range of printers?
Because they're always jammin'!
Cykara, 11

What's brown and sticky?
A stick!
Ted, 8

What did the dog say to the tree?
Bark!
Lalita, 11

MORE QUICK GAGS
from Billy Whizz

I went to the corner shop – and bought four corners!

Then I went to the paper shop – but it had blown away!

I wanted to buy a camouflage t-shirt, but I couldn't see any!

I saw an advert from someone selling a dead budgie. It wasn't going cheap.

I bought a paper shirt, but it was no good – in fact it was tearable!

Once you've seen one shopping centre, you've seen a mall.

PLUG GAGS

How ugly is Plug?
Well, he has to sneak
up on mirrors!

How ugly is Plug?
When he chops
onions, the
onions cry!

How ugly is Plug?
He gets ALL
the sweets at
Halloween!

Someone gave Plug a nasty look. **Plug said, 'Thanks, but I've got one already!'**

My girlfriend's got a complexion like a peach. **She's all yellow and fuzzy!**

Plug is actually dark and handsome. **When it's dark, he's handsome!**

They broke the mould when they made Plug. **Actually, they may have broken it before they made him!**

What's the first thing you notice about Plug? **Depends which way he's facing!**

75

Calamity James'

Top 13 Unfortunate Doctor, Doctor Jokes (Part Two)

James went to the doctor and was told to lie on the couch. He asked, 'What for?' The doctor said, 'I just swept the floor!'

'Doctor, doctor, I keep thinking I'm a comedian.'
'You must be joking!'

'Doctor, doctor, I keep thinking I'm a car.'
'You must be going round the bend!'

'Doctor, doctor, I keep thinking I'm a bridge.'
'What's come over you?'
'Two buses, three cars and a lorry!'

Olive the Cook says ...
Eat up, it's good for you!

'Yuk, my plate's wet!'
'Don't be cheeky –
that's the soup!'

Olive's food is very tasty.
A week after eating
some, you can still
taste it!

I'm not saying Olive's food
is bad, but she serves
gravy by the slice!

Why is Olive cruel?
Because she batters
fish, beats eggs and
whips cream!

'Olive, this food tastes funny!'
'Then why aren't you laughing?'

'Olive, can you tell me what this food is?'
'Why do you want to know?'
'I don't, but I think my doctor is going to ask me pretty soon!'

'I thought there was going to be a choice for lunch. You've only got liver sausage and mashed turnips.'
'Yes, and that's the choice – take it or leave it!'

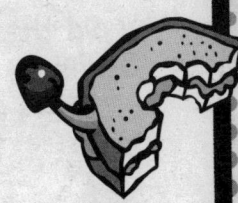

'Olive, there's a worm on my plate!'
'Don't be cheeky, that's a sausage!'

'Teacher, are caterpillars poisonous?'
'Not usually. Why do you ask?'
'There was one on your salad!'

'Ewww! This coffee tastes like soap!'
'That's not coffee, Teacher, it's tea. The coffee tastes like glue!'

BANANAMAN'S
Further Fruity Funnies

What is the most romantic fruit salad?
A date with a peach!

Where do baby apes sleep?
In apricots!

Why did the tomato blush?
Because he saw the salad dressing!

Why didn't the banana snore?
It didn't want to wake up the rest of the bunch!

What fruit teases you?
A banaa-naa na naa-naa!

How do you make a banana milkshake?
Sneak up on some banana milk and yell 'BOO!'

Knock, knock!
Who's there?
Orange.
Orange who?
Orange you glad
to see me?

What's square
and green?
A banana in disguise!

What's small, round and
giggles non-stop?
A tickled onion!

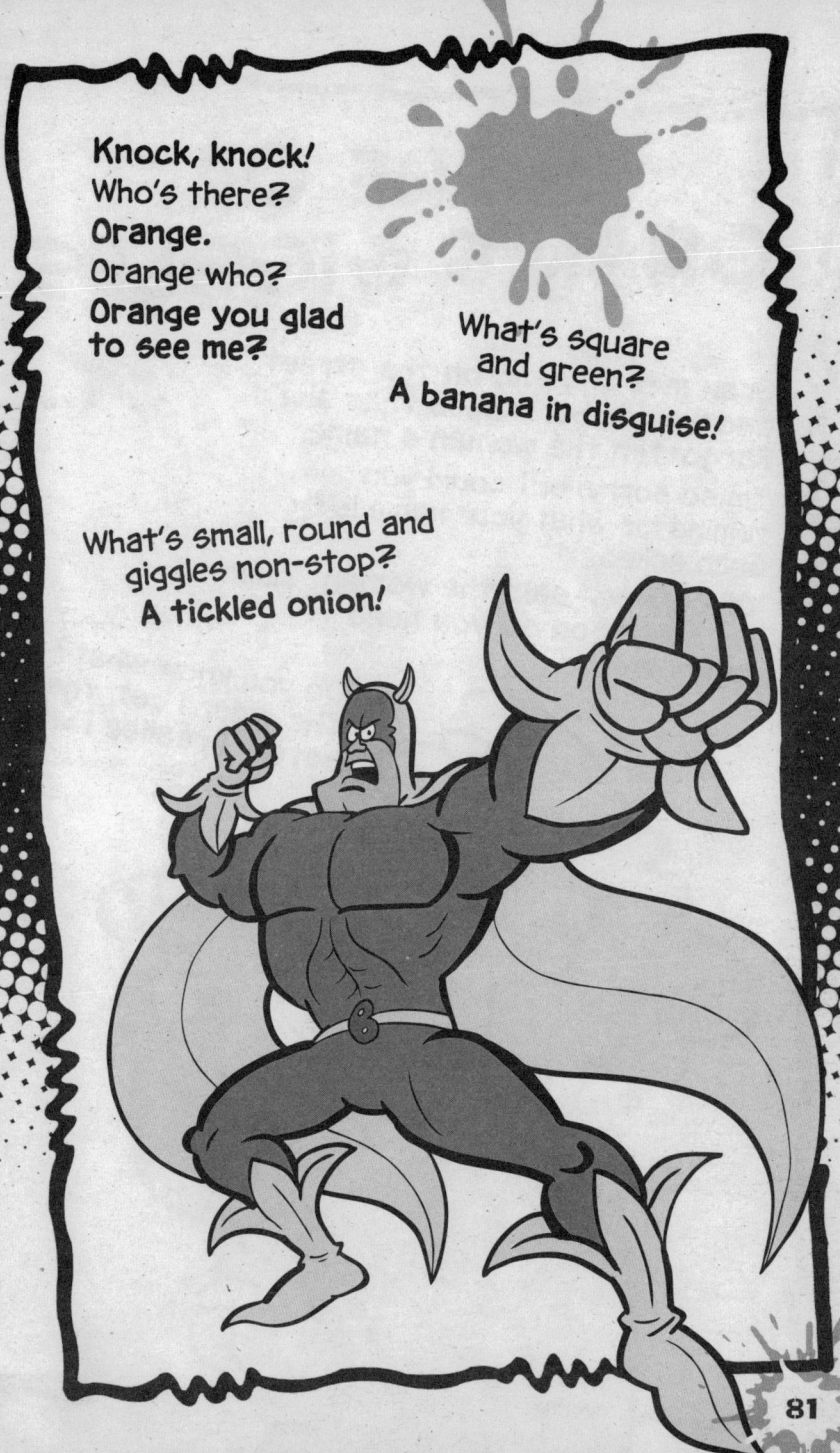

MORE OF GRAN'S GIGGLES

Gran met a friend on the street and was embarrassed that she'd forgotten the woman's name.

'I'm so sorry, but could you remind me what your name is?' Gran asked.

'Of course,' said the woman. 'Umm . . . how soon do you need to know?'

'Do you know what? The older I get, the better I realise I was!'

Why are Gran's teeth like stars?

Because they come out at night!

When Gran was little, she only had a bath once a month.

Whether she needed it or not!

When does Gran goes to bed?

Three hours after falling asleep on the sofa!

Gran has an alarm clock on the back of her motorbike.

That way she gets everywhere ahead of time!

What's grey and goes up, down, up, down?

Gran on a trampoline!

How many grans does it take to change a lightbulb?

Two. One to change the bulb, and one to go on about how much better lightbulbs were in the old days!

RASHER'S
Second Slice of Bacony Banter

What do sick pigs
get from the
doctor?
Oinkment!

What do you get when
a pig mixes colours?
Pigment!

Why should you never
tell a pig a secret?
**Because they love
to squeal!**

Why did the farmer call
his pig 'Ink'?
**Because it always ran
out of the pen!**

Why do pigs run into trees?
**To shake out
the alligators.**

I've never seen an alligator
in a tree before.

**That's because the pigs
do such a good job!**

What do you call a pig that knows karate?
A pork chop!

Sam, 8

What do you get when you cross a dinosaur with a pig?
Jurassic pork!

What happened to the pig that lost its voice?
It became disgruntled!

How did the pig get to hospital?
In a hambulance!

Madeline, 9

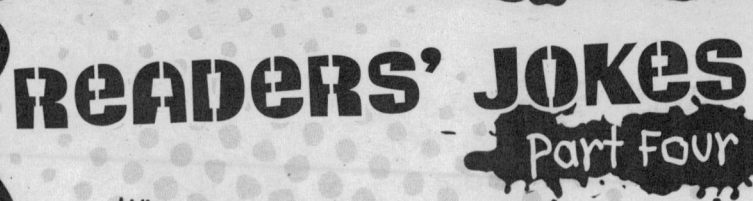

READERS' JOKES
Part Four

What do you get if you cross a sheep with a kangaroo?

A woolly jumper!

Natasha, 7

Knock, knock!
Who's there?
Dwayne.
Dwayne who?
Dwayne the bath, I'm dwowning!

Lorna, 7

Why is tap-dancing so dangerous?

Because you might fall in the sink!

Michael, 9

What did one tomato say to the other tomato?

You go on and I'll ketchup later!

Odysseus, 4

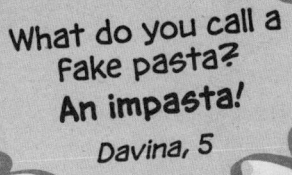

What do you call a
fake pasta?
An impasta!
Davina, 5

Did you hear about
the crazy robot?
**He went nuts
and bolts!**
Jim, 7

What did the traffic
light say to the cars?
**Don't look,
I'm changing!**
Sameeha, 8

What is a sea monster's
favourite lunch?
Fish and ships!
Theo, 6

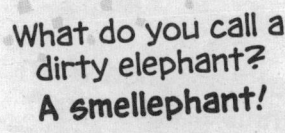

What do you call a
dirty elephant?
A smellephant!
Evie, 8

87

MORE MENACE FUNNIES

'Why are you always so dirty, Dennis?'
'Well, I'm a lot nearer the ground than you are, Mum!'

Dennis first met Pie Face when they crashed their karts together.
They met by accident!

Dennis hates pulling his kart back up hills.
It's such a drag!

What happened when Dennis and Gnasher drove a magic tractor down the road?
It turned into a field!

Xavier, 7

Did Mum and Dad get any peace and quiet when Dennis was little?
Only after son-down!

What is Dennis the Menace's favourite snack? Beanos on toast!

Cordelia, 11

What did the grape do when Dennis trod on it? It let out a little wine!

Isaac, 4

GNASHTASTIC!

What happens when it
rains cats and dogs?
**You can step in
a poodle!**

What is the only dog
you can eat?
A hot dog!

When I met my friend's dog for the first time I asked her name. She told me, 'Whisper'. So I asked again in a quiet voice, 'What's your dog's name?'

What do you call a family of young dogs who have come in from the snow?
Slush puppies!

How do you feel if you cross a sheepdog with a melon?
Melon-collie!

'My dog has no nose!'
'How does he smell?'
'Terrible!'

Elsa, 6

What kind of dog does Dracula have?
A bloodhound!

What is a scientist's favourite dog?
A lab!

Ben, 11

The Bash Street Kids'
classroom crackers

What word
is always
spelled wrongly?
'Wrongly'!

Why was the
headmaster worried?
Because there were
too many rulers
in school!

Teacher: 'Why were you late?'
Toots: 'Sorry, Teacher, I overslept.'
Teacher: 'You mean you need to
sleep at home too?'

Why didn't the skeleton go to the school dance?
He didn't have any body to take!

Why is Russia a very fast country?
Because the people are always Russian!

What is a snake's favourite subject?
Hisssstory!

Why did Fatty eat his homework?
Because Teacher said it was a piece of cake!

Why did Smiffy throw his watch out of the window?
He wanted to see time fly!

More Little Fun With
LITTLE PLUM

Plum told the Chief he should to exercise by walking five miles every day.

A month later, the Chief was much fitter – and 150 miles away!

Two cowboys staggered out of the zoo covered in scratches.

'You know what?' said one. 'That there lion dancing ain't as much fun as we were told!'

A dog limped into a saloon on crutches and announced,

'I'm lookin' for the man who shot my paw!'

Did you hear about the cowboy who dressed from head to toe in brown paper clothes?

He was arrested for rustling!

A man is smoking a cigar and blowing smoke rings when the Chief storms up to him.

'Listen, buddy,' he growls. 'If you don't stop calling me names, there'll be trouble!'

Is it simple to use a lasso?

It's easy to pick up, but you have to learn the ropes!

Did you hear about the cowboy who was good at making flatpack furniture?

He was quick on the drawer!

TWANG!

Weedy Walter's LOVELY LAUGHS

What's a snowman's favourite flower?
A freeze-ia!

What do you get if you divide the circumference of a pumpkin by its diameter?
Pumpkin pi!

Knock, knock!
Who's there?
Lettuce.
Lettuce who?
Lettuce in, it's cold out here!

What do you call a
popular perfume?
A best-smeller!

What's a frog's
favourite flower?
A croak-us!

Why can't you iron a
four-leaf clover?
**Because you shouldn't
press your luck!**

Walter fancies
opening a flower shop
when he's older.
**He's heard business
is blooming!**

Why is the letter A
like a flower?
**Because it has a
bee coming after it!**

READERS' JOKES
Part Five

What do you call
six ducks in a box?
**A box of
quackers!**
Katherine, 6

What is the
difference between
origami and grandpa
passing wind?
**One's the art of the
fold, and the other
one's the fart of
the old!**
Fred, 8

What do you call
a donkey with
three legs?
A wonkey!
Katy, 4

How do you make a
sausage roll?
Push it down a hill!
James, 8

Knock, knock!
Who's there?
Panther.
Panther who?
Panth or no panth, I'm going thwimming!
Charlotte, 7

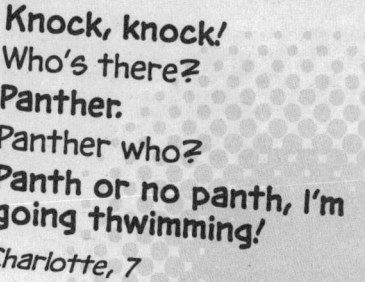

Why did the baker have dirty hands?
Because he kneaded a poo!
Johnny, 6

What do you call a skeleton in a cupboard?
Hide and seek champion 1985!
Liam, 2½

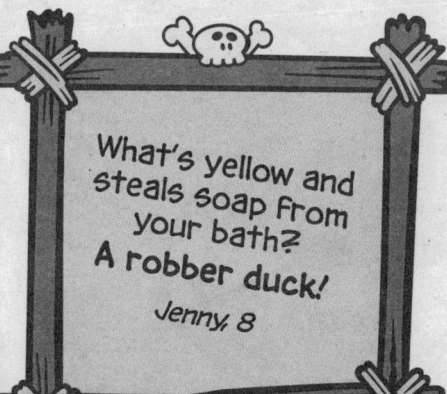

What's yellow and steals soap from your bath?
A robber duck!
Jenny, 8

What do you call a fish with no eyes?
Fsh!
Corin, 7

Calamity James'

Even Unluckier Doctor Doctor Jokes!

'Doctor, doctor, I keep thinking I'm a tennis racket.'

'Don't worry – you're just highly strung!'

'Doctor, doctor, I keep thinking I'm a doorknob.'

'All right, don't fly off the handle!'

'Doctor, doctor, I keep thinking I'm a trunk.'
'I've never seen a case like yours before!'

'Doctor, doctor, I'm only four feet tall.'
'You'll just have to be a little patient!'

'Doctor, doctor, I'm worried about my insomnia.'
'Don't lose any sleep over it!'

'Doctor, doctor, I'm just not myself.'
'Yes – I noticed the improvement!'

'Doctor, doctor, I think I need glasses.'
'You certainly do . . . this is a restaurant!'

'Doctor, doctor, I can't stop climbing mountains.'
'Relax, we'll soon have you in peak condition!'

THE 3 BEARS'
Fuzzy Funnies

What do you call a
bear with no teeth?
A gummy bear!

How do you start a
baby bear race?
'Ready, teddy, go!'

What do you call a
wet bear?
A drizzly bear!

What kind of
money do polar
bears use?
Ice lolly!

Why don't bears wear socks?
They prefer to go around in their bear feet!

A polar bear goes into a café and asks, 'Can I have . . . a cup of tea please?'
The owner gets the tea but is curious. 'Why the big pause?'
'Don't know,' says the polar bear. 'I've always had them!'

What does Biffo do when it rains?
He gets wet!

Can Biffo stand any more of these jokes?
Bearly!

'What's the difference between a bear and a postbox?'
'I don't know.'
'Then I'm not giving you any letters to post!'

THE NUMSKULLS'
Extra Body Groaners!

It's easy using deodorant. **No sweat!**

People are jealous of how Flexible I am. **I have to watch my back!**

Police Finally captured the blond burglar with a box-shaped head. **They caught him fair and square!**

What's the best cure for sea-sickness? **Sit under a tree!**

Why was the nose tired? **Because it had been running all day!**

Why did the man with one hand cross the road?
To get to the second-hand shop!

How does the man in the moon cut his hair?
Eclipse it!

When are eyes not eyes?
When the wind makes them water!

What do hippies do?
They hold your leggies on!

Some people are made upside-down.
Their noses run and their feet smell!

PUP PARADE'S
Doggy Distractions

Why don't dogs make good dancers?
Because they have two left feet!

What do you get if you cross a dog and a skunk?
Rid of the dog!

What do you call a dog with no legs?
It doesn't matter what you call him. He still won't come!

What kind of meat do
you give a stupid dog?
Chump chops!

What do you get if
you cross a dog with
a kangaroo?
**A dog that has
somewhere to carry
its own lead!**

Why do dogs run
in circles?
**Because it's hard to
run in squares!**

What do you get if
you cross a cocker
spaniel, a poodle
and a rooster?
Cockerpoodledoo!

How do you catch a
runaway dog?
**Hide behind a tree
and make a noise like
a bone!**

BILLY WHIZZ'S

Last Batch of Quick Quips!

The trouble with doing something right first time is that nobody appreciates how difficult it was.

I intend to live forever. So far, so good.

Some people cause happiness wherever they go. Others cause it **whenever** they go!

I used to be indecisive. Now I'm not so sure.

When tempted to fight fire with fire, remember that the Fire Brigade usually uses water.

Have you ever thought – forty years from now, LOTS of grannies will have tattoos.

They say that money talks – but all mine ever says is 'Goodbye.'

It's amazing – the amount of news that happens every day always just fits the newspaper.

I like work. It fascinates me. I can sit and look at it for hours!

OH NO! IT'S BEA'S GUFF GAGS!

After a day dealing with Bea's nappies, Mum and Dad were completely pooped!

How does Bea make a tissue dance?

She puts a little boogie in it!

Mum and Dad spent Bea's first year teaching her to walk and talk – and ever since, they've been hoping she'll keep still and be quiet!

What do you get if you sit under a cow?

A pat on the head!

Aidan, 7

What are invisible and smell of carrots?

Rabbit farts!

Mum found Bea chewing on a slug. 'That's disgusting! What on earth does that taste like?' Bea thought for a moment. 'Worms,' she replied!

Why did the lobster blush? Because the sea-weed!

What's brown and sounds like a bell? 'Dung!'

What animal lives in the sea and goes to the loo eight times a day? An octo-poos!

Eve, 5¾

PHAAART!

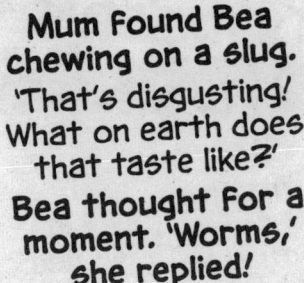

ROGER THE DODGER'S
ROTTEN RIDDLES

What do you call a boomerang that won't come back?
A stick!

What has holes in the top, bottom and both sides, but still holds water?
A sponge!

Poor people have it. Rich people need it. If you eat it you die. What is it?
Nothing!

There are thirty people under one umbrella. How many get wet?
None – it isn't raining!

What can you catch but not throw?
A cold!

What gets smaller the more you put into it?
A hole in the ground!

What can travel around the world without leaving the corner?
A stamp!

What is lighter than a feather, but not even Pansy Potter could hold it for five minutes?
Her breath!

What do you call an igloo with no toilet?
An ig!

BANANAMAN'S
Supergags!

What's Bananaman's favourite part of a joke?
The punch-line!

What do you call a naked Bananaman?
Super-natural!

FROM A FRIEND

What has wheels and flies?
A bin lorry!

Which hero likes a bowl of minestrone for lunch?
Soup-erman!

Who flies through the sky in pants?
Pooper-man!
Elicia, 7

What do you call Batman and Robin when they've been run over?
Flatman and Ribbon!
Nathaniel, 7

Who can save the world?
Superman can, but Clark Kent!

FOOTBALL FUNNIES

Extra Time!

Did you hear about the football team who ate too much pudding?
They got jellygated!

'Can your goalkeeper jump higher than the crossbar?'
'**Of course he can - crossbars can't jump!**'

Why did the chicken get sent off?
For fowl play!

What's the best way to stay cool during a football match?
Stand near the fans!

Why couldn't the rubbish footie team have a barbecue at the end of the season?
Because they'd lost all their matches!

Big Fun With
LITTLE PLUM

Plum can't help admiring the Chief. If he doesn't, the Chief thumps him!

The word 'vegetarian' comes from an old phrase meaning 'Useless at hunting'!

What do you get when you cross a pig with a cactus?

A porkerpine!

Plum was moaning. 'I feel like thumping the Chief again.'

'What do you mean, again?'

'I felt like thumping him yesterday too!'

Why does Plum never go hungry in the desert?

Because he can always eat the sand which is there!

'Chief, I'm worried I've gone loopy – one moment I think I'm a wigwam, the next I think I'm a tepee.'

'I know your problem, Plum – you're two tents!'

What happens when the Chief passes out from eating too much curry?

He goes into a korma!

THE BASH STREET KIDS
Final Lesson!

Some people are afraid of heights, but not Smiffy.

He's afraid of widths!

Why does Plug have such big nostrils?

Because he's got big fingers!

Spotty's no good at hide-and-seek.

He's always spotted!

At what time do kids often get hurt?

Break time!

Jonty, 6

Wilfrid isn't getting anywhere with geometry.

He just keeps going in circles!

Sidney and Toots think there are three types of people in the world.

Those that can do maths, and those that can't!

Teacher: 'Well, the good news is your handwriting's getting better.'

Danny: 'So what's the bad news?'

Teacher: 'Now I can see how bad your spelling is!'

'Erbert can't understand decimal maths.

He doesn't see the point!

MINNIE'S MEGAGAGS

How does Minnie confuse an idiot?

Forty-two!

Minnie's motto? 'If it ain't broke, break it!'

Minnie doesn't understand cafés advertising 'All-Day Breakfast.'

Who has that amount of time just for breakfast?

Minnie has a good-looking, but strict, teacher.

She's easy on the eyes but tough on the pupils!

Minnie finds sleeping really easy.

She can do it with her eyes closed!

Minnie banged her left thumb yesterday.

On the other hand, she's fine!

For her birthday last year, Minnie got taken to the best restaurant in town. This year, she's hoping to be let inside!

How does Minnie take a bubble bath? She has beans for tea!

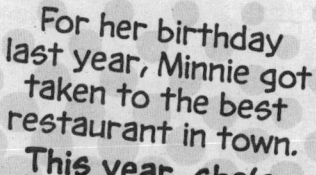

What do you call Minnie with her pockets full of sweets? Smartie pants!

GNICE ONE, GNASHER!

What dog is the best at keeping time?
A watch dog!

When is a black dog not a black dog?
When it's a greyhound!

Why did the man bring his dog to the railway station?
Because he wanted to train it!

What is more amazing that a talking dog?
A spelling bee!

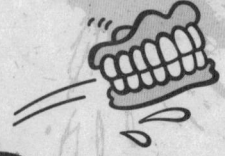

Why did the dachshund bite the woman's ankle?
Because it couldn't reach any higher!

What dog loves to take bubble baths?
A shampoodle!

Why did the snowman call his dog Frost?
Because Frost bites!

What does Gnasher like for lunch?
Bones on toast!
Campbell, 8

Dennis the Menace's
Last Laughs!

Why do children have middle names?

So they know when they're *really* in trouble!

Dennis likes Bea's unbreakable toys.

They're great for breaking things with!

How do you get Dennis out of the bath?

Turn on the water!

Dennis lost his watch, but didn't get round to looking for it.
He couldn't find the time!

What's the difference between bogies and Brussels sprouts?
Kids will eat bogies!

How does Mum open a jar with a stuck lid?
She leaves it on the table and tells Dennis not to touch it!

'That's a cool chair, Gran!'
'Yeah, I know. It rocks!'

'Dad, when I grow up I want to drive a tank!'
'Well, I definitely won't stand in your way!'

When is the only time Dennis washes his ears?
When he eats a slice of watermelon!